KV-197-826

All Aboard the Ark

Sheila Lane and Marion Kemp

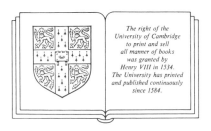

The right of the
University of Cambridge
to print and sell
all manner of books
was granted by
Henry VIII in 1534.
The University has printed
and published continuously
since 1584.

CAMBRIDGE UNIVERSITY PRESS
Cambridge
New York   New Rochelle
Melbourne   Sydney

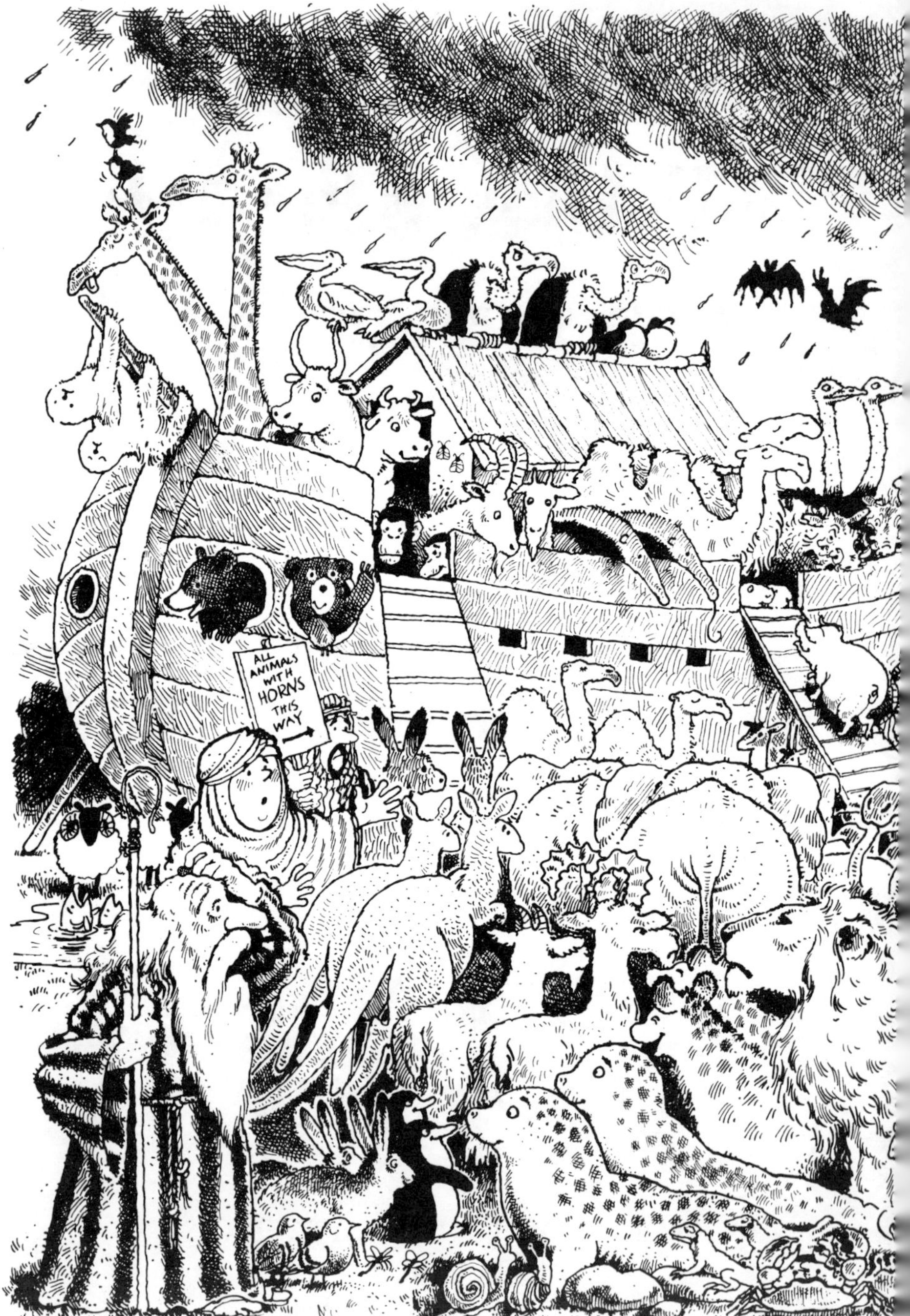
ALL ANIMALS WITH HORNS THIS WAY

All Aboard the Ark

This book is about how Noah and his family rescued and cared for the animals during the Great Flood.

The book begins with all the animals hurrying to climb onto the Ark during the 'All Aboard' song. The Noahs have problems in settling everyone down, so they suggest that the animals should tell each other stories, in order to pass the time. The stories are told as three plays, but the animals become very troublesome and noisy. The book ends with the Noahs tricking the animals into being quiet and everyone joining in a sing-along before they reach dry land.

The characters who take part in the plays are the **Playmakers.** The Noah family and the animals who watch the three plays are the **Playwatchers.**

Contents

PLAYWATCHERS

All Aboard

The Noah family

NOAH

MRS NOAH

HAM

HAM'S WIFE

SHEM

SHEM'S WIFE

JAPHET

JAPHET'S WIFE

The 'All Aboard' animals

FIRST HEDGEHOG

SECOND HEDGEHOG

FIRST MOUSE

SECOND MOUSE

FIRST HAMSTER

SECOND HAMSTER

FIRST SEA-LION

SECOND SEA-LION

FIRST CAT

SECOND CAT

FIRST DOG

SECOND DOG

FIRST ELEPHANT

SECOND ELEPHANT

FIRST GIRAFFE

SECOND GIRAFFE

Other animals

NOAH *and his family* (MRS NOAH, HAM, SHEM, JAPHET *and their* WIVES) *'build' the Ark shape (see p. 69) as they sing the first verse of the 'All Aboard' song (see p. 68 for tune). They put up notices (see p. 72).*

1 The Noahs built a giant Ark,   (*A few animals*
  Rock an' roll an' rock.   *begin to*
  Gobble, growl, quack and quark,   *assemble.*)
  Rock an' roll an' rock.

Chorus
Rock an' roll   (*More animals*
Aboard the floating Zoo,   *assemble outside*
Rock an' roll   *the Ark and join*
Aboard the floating Zoo.   *in singing.*)

2 The animals came in two by two,   (*Some animals*
  Rock an' roll an' rock.   *enter the Ark.*
  The Noahs cried, 'What shall we do?'   *The Noah family*
  Rock an' roll an' rock.   *looks worried.*)

Chorus   (NOAH *goes out.*)

3 The animals came in four by four,   (*More animals*
  Rock an' roll an' rock.   *enter the Ark.*
  The Noahs cried, 'Let's shut the door!'   *The Noahs look*
  Rock an' roll an' rock.   *very alarmed.*)

Chorus

(When the singing stops, the Noah family comes forward to the inside of the ropes.)

ALL NOAHS   No more! No more! Let's shut the door!

(NOAH *returns carrying three more notices.*)

NOAH   No! No! They must all come in. We must get them properly organised. Now, Ham! Read this. (*He holds up a notice.*)

HAM   "ALL HEAVY ANIMALS THIS WAY." That's a good idea, father. Now then . . . (*shouting*) All heavy animals this way. Come on, you elephants!

FIRST ELEPHANT   All right! Elephants can read, you know.

SECOND ELEPHANT   And elephants never forget!

HAM'S WIFE   All giraffes! This way!

FIRST GIRAFFE   We're not heavy animals.

SECOND GIRAFFE   We're just tall.

HAM   Don't start arguing. You'll all be much better off if you do as you're told.

NOAH   Shem! This one is for you. (*He holds up a notice.*)

SHEM   "ALL ANIMALS WITH HORNS THIS WAY." Come on you horny beasts. Cows! Reindeer! Rhinos! Over here!

SHEM'S WIFE   What about the hedgehogs, Shem?

SHEM	Ah yes! This notice should say: ALL ANIMALS WITH HORNS OR PRICKLES WHICH MAKE OTHER PEOPLE UNCOMFORTABLE, THIS WAY!
FIRST HEDGEHOG	We don't make people uncomfortable unless they attack us.
SECOND HEDGEHOG	Why is that man saying nasty things about us?
FIRST HEDGEHOG	People do!
NOAH	Japhet! You must stop the fish from coming aboard. (*He hands a notice to Japhet.*)
JAPHET	"ALL FISH MUST MAKE THEIR OWN ARRANGEMENTS!" This notice should say: ALL CREATURES THAT CAN SWIM MUST MAKE THEIR OWN ARRANGEMENTS.
JAPHET'S WIFE	In that case, we won't have any sea-lions. Go back, sea-lions! You can swim along behind.
FIRST SEA-LION	But you let the land lions on board.
SECOND SEA-LION	So it's not fair to keep us out.
JAPHET	You can swim.
FIRST SEA-LION	But we're mammals. Anyone will tell you that.
SECOND SEA-LION	Tell him we must have nice rocks to rest on.
FIRST SEA-LION	Please let her come on board. She won't take up much room.

SECOND SEA-LION	I can't go without you, dear.
FIRST SEA-LION	Shh! I'll slip in on the other side. Keep talking.
SECOND SEA-LION	All right! (*loudly*) What shall I do? I'm not up to long distance swimming these days.
JAPHET	Oh, all right then! Come along.
MRS NOAH	Now animals, are you sitting comfortably?
FIRST MOUSE	I'm not!
SECOND MOUSE	I'm sitting very uncomfortably.
FIRST HAMSTER	It's this hedgehog!
SECOND HAMSTER	We mice and hamsters have such tender skins, Mrs Noah. Please give us a place away from the hedgehogs.
MRS NOAH	Poor little things! Come along over here. This is a nice, quiet corner. Move over, Cat.
FIRST MOUSE	Cat! Cat! Don't say that!
SECOND MOUSE	Oh, Mrs Noah! We can't sit by a cat!
FIRST CAT	We cats aren't moving.
SECOND CAT	We like this nice, quiet corner.
FIRST DOG	Come over here by us . . . Puss!
SECOND DOG	We'll lick your fur. We'll make you purr!
MRS NOAH	Yes, that's what I'll do. I'll put you two cats over here by the dogs.

FIRST CAT	It's not fair! We were here first.
SECOND CAT	Besides! Dogs chase cats!
MRS NOAH	What nonsense! We're ALL FRIENDS on the Ark. Now! I do believe everyone's sitting comfortably at last.
NOAH	At last! Now we can go and get some supper. Come along, family.
	(*All Noah family, except Mrs Noah, goes out.*)
MRS NOAH	Now animals! No quarrelling! Particularly you dogs and cats!
FIRST CAT	Dogs and cats always quarrel.
SECOND CAT	Well . . . nearly always . . . except in stories.
MRS NOAH	Stories! That's a good idea, Puss! Now, you come and tell the animals a story while I go and help with the supper.
FIRST CAT	What kind of story?
MRS NOAH	A story about . . . let me see . . . a story about a cat and a dog . . . and lots of other animals . . . with a happy ending. (*She goes out.*)
SECOND CAT	Let me think . . . Well . . . Once upon a time there was a cat, a dog and . . . a donkey . . . who all lived together on a farm.
	Look! Here they come!

Here begins the story of The Donkey's Band.

The Donkey's Band

Playmakers

Animals
DONKEY – Moke
CAT – Whiskers
DOG – Growler

COCK
HEN
TURKEY – Gobbler
DUCK

BULL – Benjamin
COW
PIG
GOAT

Other animals

Robbers
BOSS
DUD
STUMP
GRUMP
JEM
CLEM
HANK
FRANK

Other robbers

The Donkey's Band

DONKEY, CAT *and* DOG *are hurrying down the road away from the farm.*

DONKEY Come on, Growler! Move a bit faster!

DOG I'm coming as fast as I can.

DONKEY Then move a bit faster!

DOG Don't keep on at me.

CAT Don't grumble at him, Moke. Let him sit down and rest for a bit.

DONKEY All right! All right! We're a long way from the farm now, so we'll all sit down.

CAT After all, Farmer is talking of getting rid of the three of us because we're old and slow.

DOG It's too bad!

DONKEY When you're old and slow, my friends, it's OUT!

CAT I want a home where I can stay IN! I want a home where I can sit by the fire with a saucer of milk, instead of hunting for mice all night.

DOG Me too! I want to stay in at night.

DONKEY And no more carts to pull to market! I want a nice, warm home, and nice brown sugar, and . . .

CAT And a nice lot of money to buy the sugar with! Have you thought of that, Moke?

DONKEY Don't worry, Whiskers! Trust your old friend Moke. This is my plan . . . We will all go into the town together and become town musicians.

CAT That won't help us to get money to buy the things we need.

DONKEY Don't worry, Whiskers! People will give us money when they hear us sing. You've got a wonderful voice. We've all heard you sitting on the barn roof singing to the moon at night!

DOG What about me?

DONKEY You have a fine, deep voice, Growler. And as for me . . .

DOG What about you?

CAT You have a terrible voice, Moke. Everyone says that.

DONKEY I know I haven't a true singing voice, but . . .

CAT It's a terrible voice, Moke. People will run away if they hear you sing.

DOG They will run out of town!
Listen! I can hear someone running now.

DONKEY It sounds like some of our farmyard friends. I do believe I can hear Cock's voice.

CAT Look! Here come Cock, Hen, Turkey and Duck.
(*Enter* COCK, HEN, TURKEY *and* DUCK.)

DONKEY What's the matter? Why are you all crowing and squawking and gobbling and quacking like that?

COCK Why? Because Sunday visitors are coming tomorrow and Farmer's Wife has ordered Cook to make me into soup. Me!

HEN And I can't stay at the farm without Cock.

DONKEY But why are you and Duck so upset, Gobbler?

TURKEY Christmas is coming! Christmas is coming!

DUCK And then it will be our turn. Cook will put Turkey and me in the pot.

DONKEY Then you'd better join us. Cat and Dog and I are running away because we heard Farmer talking of getting rid of us.

BIRDS	Where are you going? Where are you going?
DONKEY	We're going to town together to become town musicians. We were just making some plans when we heard your voices. Ah! Voices! We need your voices, my fine feathered friends.
CAT	People are going to pay to hear us sing. In this way we shall earn our living.
DOG	I have a fine, deep voice.
COCK	As everyone knows, I have a voice of the finest quality. Don't I practise every morning and wake everyone up?
HEN	You do, Cock! You do!
TURKEY	Can you make use of my fine gobble, gobble?
DUCK	And my quack, quack?
DONKEY	Of course! Of course! As the conductor of the Animal Band, I can make use of you all. Let's practise.
COCK	I'll start everything off. After all, I'm quite used to doing that. I'll sing my cock-a-doodle-doo and then everyone else can join in.
DONKEY	Now look here, Cock. I'm in charge of this band. In fact, I was the conductor until you birds came along.
COCK	All right! All right! (*quietly*) Don't some of these old animals get touchy! (*loudly*) I was just offering my services, that's all.
DONKEY	All right, then. Now . . . Watch my front leg and join in when I give the signal. We'll begin with a solo from Cock.
COCK	What a brilliant idea!
DONKEY	One! Two! Three! (COCK *begins. Others are brought in until all are singing together.*)

DONKEY	Stop! STOP! S T O P! How on earth can I stop them? STOP!
COCK	What are you singing, Moke?
DONKEY	I'm not singing. I'm shouting STOP!
COCK	Then you should stop conducting. How are we to know that you want us to stop when you're still waving your front leg in the air like that? You must stop conducting and say CUT!
DONKEY	All right! Cut, everyone! CUT! (*Animals stop singing.*) That's better . . . Now I can hear myself think!
CAT	Were we good, Moke?
ALL	Were we good? Were we good?
DONKEY	Well . . . (*doubtfully*) Perhaps you need a bit more practice.
COCK	Perhaps we need better voices! Dog is terrible. He's just a growler.
DOG	That's too bad! I do my best and then you get at me.
DONKEY	No we don't, Growler. Oh! Sorry! I didn't mean to call you that.
COCK	I know! As we are supposed to be a band, Dog can beat time on the floor with his tail.
DOG	I'll be a drum. Good! I'll be a drum.
COCK	But we must have some deep voices too. Ah! I know who we need. We need Benjamin.
HEN	Benjamin Bull?
TURKEY	Benjamin Bull! Benjamin Bull!
DUCK	What about Cow . . . and Pig . . . and Goat? They have deep voices.

DONKEY	That's a good idea! They're in the field down the road. Go and call them, Growler. Go on . . . Hurry!
DOG	All right! Don't keep on at me! (*He goes out.*)
COCK	Another brilliant idea, Moke! I can see that you are well suited to be the leader of this band.
CAT	Listen! Benjamin is coming. I can hear his bellow.
HEN	I can hear Cow.
TURKEY	And Pig, and Goat.
	(*Enter* DOG, *followed by* BULL, COW, PIG *and* GOAT.)
DOG	I've got Bull . . . and Cow . . . and Pig . . . and Goat.
BULL	Now then, Moke! What's this all about? I don't like being disturbed like this.
COW	Why are all of you out here at this time of night?
PIG	You birds should be asleep.
GOAT	What's it all about?
DONKEY	We three heard Farmer talking of getting rid of us because we're old and slow. So we're running away.
COCK	And we birds heard Farmer's Wife ordering Cook to make me into soup.
HEN	And I can't stay at the farm without Cock.
TURKEY	Christmas is coming! Christmas is coming!
DUCK	So it will be our turn next to be put in the pot.
BULL	This is a bad business, a bad business!
COCK	And I shouldn't be surprised if your turn isn't coming, Benjamin.
DONKEY	It's been put about that Farmer is getting rid of all you animals soon.

BULL, COW, PIG, GOAT	Us! Us! Not us!
BULL	What are you intending to do, Donkey?
DONKEY	We are planning to go into the town and become town musicians.
CAT	People will give us money when they hear us sing.
DOG	I am going to play the drum with my tail.
COCK	You four had better come with us while you can. Besides, we chose you because you have such fine voices.
DONKEY	So will you join our band?
CAT AND DOG	Say yes! Say yes!
BULL, COW, PIG, GOAT	Yes! Yes! We will!
DONKEY	Let's practise then. Watch my front leg and join in when I give the signal. We begin with a solo from Cock. One! Two! Three!
	(COCK *sings. Others are brought in.*)
DONKEY	Stop! STOP! Oh dear! That's not the way to stop them. I must stop conducting and shout, 'Cut!' Cut! CUT! (*Band stops.*)
CAT	Were we good, Moke?
ALL	Were we good? Were we good?
DONKEY	Much better! Much better! Now . . . we'll walk towards the town and play as we go. Come along! Get into line! Follow me . . . One! Two! Three!
	(*Animals go off still singing as they circle back of arena and re-enter from other side,* DOG *at rear banging tail.*)

BULL	Stop! Stop all of you! STOP!
	(*All stop, except* MOKE, *who goes on conducting.*)
	Stop, Moke! STOP!
COW	What's the matter, Benjamin?
GOAT	What is it, Benjamin?
PIG	What can you see?
BULL	(*pointing*) There's a light over there!
COCK	If there's a light, there must be a house.
HEN	If there's a house, I can rest my poor little legs.
TURKEY	If there's a house, there may be some food.
DUCK	If there's a house, there may be some water.
CAT	What a lot of parrots these birds are!
COCK	Watch your tongue, Whiskers! I'm going in.
BULL	Hang on! Don't rush it! A house can mean people. People can mean enemies.
DONKEY	That's true. I vote that Cat should go and find out who is there.
CAT	All right! I'll jump up the tree outside the window and look in. (*She goes out.*)
DOG	Take care, Whiskers! Take care!
BULL	There's trouble ahead. I feel it in my bones. I wish I hadn't mentioned that light. A light means people . . . People can mean . . .
	(*Enter* CAT.)
CAT	It's robbers! It's robbers!
ALL	ROBBERS!
BULL	Ssh! Ssh! Too late! They've heard us! They're coming! Quick! Come on . . . Over here!
	(ANIMAL BAND *goes out. Enter Robbers:* BOSS *and* DUD, *followed by* STUMP *and* GRUMP, JEM *and* CLEM, HANK *and* FRANK.)

19

BOSS	Hallo! Hallo! Hallo! If my big ears don't deceive me, there are strangers about.
DUD	(*looking around*) No, Boss. There's no-one here.
BOSS	Is Boss ever wrong in these matters, Dud?
DUD	No, Boss! No!
BOSS	Then scout round, lads! (*pointing*) Stump and Grump, go that way.
STUMP, GRUMP	Aye! Aye! Boss! (*They go.*)
BOSS	Jem and Clem! (*pointing*) Over there!
JEM, CLEM	As you say, Boss! (*They go.*)
BOSS	And Hank and Frank! (*pointing*) Over there!
HANK	Oh no, Boss!
FRANK	Not over THERE!
BOSS	And why not?
HANK, FRANK	We. . .'re . . . sc. . .ar. . .ed!
BOSS	Call yourselves robbers and act scared! GET OVER THERE!
HANK, FRANK	B . . . b . . . b . . . ut.
BOSS	There are two of you, aren't there?
HANK, FRANK	Yes, Boss.
BOSS	So. . .! (*He moves towards them, shaking his fist.*)
HANK, FRANK	OK, Boss! OK! (*They go.*)
BOSS	Call themselves robbers!
DUD	Call themselves robbers!
BOSS	What are you going to do?
DUD	I'll stay with you, Boss!
	(*Enter* STUMP *and* GRUMP.)
STUMP	No-one there, Boss.
GRUMP	No-one there at all.
	(*Enter* JEM *and* CLEM.)

JEM There's no-one about, Boss.

CLEM No-one at all.
(*Enter* HANK *and* FRANK.)

HANK We looked, Boss.

FRANK We looked EVERYWHERE, Boss.

BOSS OK! OK! Well, maybe I was mistaken. Maybe my big ears did deceive me.

DUD Can we get back to the grub, Boss?

BOSS OK! OK! Everybody in!
(*All go.*)

DONKEY (*entering on side of arena away from robbers' house*) Ssh! Ssh! Come out quietly, everyone. Not a sound! Over here now.

(ANIMAL BAND *follows Donkey.*)

BULL I told you! I told you! A house means people and people mean enemies. We shall have to go on to the town.

COCK What nonsense! What rubbish! What balderdash! I've never seen such scared robbers in all my life.

DONKEY That Boss robber wasn't scared.

BULL And there were eight of them altogether. I counted.

COCK And there are eleven of us! So!

DONKEY So what?

COCK So we must drive them out of their little house and get it for ourselves.

BULL But how?

COCK We'll frighten them out. Don't you realise that together we can scare them away from this place for ever. Then we can have the house for our headquarters.

DONKEY Oh, how lovely! A headquarters for the Animal Band.

COCK That's right. And remember everyone – they've got food in there.

ALL (*softly*) Food! Food! Food!

BULL But how can we get them out?

COCK Why! Sing them out, of course! When they hear us sing they'll run a mile! Don't you agree, Moke? You know you have brilliant ideas.

DONKEY Of course! Of course! When they hear us sing, they'll run a mile. Now let's make our group over there and when all the robbers have run out, we'll run in!

BULL All right! I'll go in last because I'm the strongest. Then I can bolt the door.

COCK Good for you, Bull!

DONKEY Now, are you all ready?
One! Two! Three! Sing!

(*All* ROBBERS *run into centre of arena, then rush wildly about.* ANIMALS *move off quickly into the robbers' house.*)

BOSS (*to nobody in particular*) Take that! And that! And that!

(*All* ROBBERS *hit out wildly.*)

DUD And you take that! (*hitting Hank accidentally*)

HANK Come on, Frank! We're not stopping here!

FRANK I'm coming!
(FRANK *and* HANK *go.*)

STUMP, GRUMP Come on! Let's go! (*They go.*)

BOSS No! Come back!

22

JEM, CLEM	We're off! (*They go.*)
BOSS	Come back, you cowards!
DUD	I'll get them back, Boss. (*He goes.*)
BOSS	And that's the last I'll see of him and the rest of them. COWARDS! (*He goes out shouting,* 'Cowards! Cowards!')
	(COCK *puts head out.*)
COCK	So my little plan worked! (*Sings to the 'All Aboard' tune:*) We've scared them off with music's charm, Cock-a-doodle-doo. And now we'll live here free from harm, Cock-a-doodle-doo.

(*Chorus from off stage by* ANIMAL BAND)
Free from harm,
Inside the robbers' house.
Free from harm,
Inside the robbers' house.

END OF FIRST PLAY

 **PLAYWATCHERS**

All Aboard

Applause from 'All Aboard' animals.

FIRST ELEPHANT	Come on everyone! Let's have our own concert. I'll conduct with my trunk. One! Two! Three!
	(Uproar, as animals make their own sounds. Enter HAM *and* WIFE.)
HAM	What a terrible noise!
HAM'S WIFE	Stop! Stop at once!
	(Animals quieten down.)
FIRST ELEPHANT	We were only making a band like the animals in the story. Listen to my fine voice! *(trumpets)*
SECOND ELEPHANT	And mine is even better! *(joins in)*
ALL ANIMALS	And mine is better still! *(All join in again.)*
HAM	*(putting hands over ears.)* Stop! STOP! S T O P! You've got terrible voices! And you're making a terrible noise!
	(Animals quieten down.)
HAM'S WIFE	We can't have a noise like that on the Ark!
FIRST ELEPHANT	Why not?
SECOND ELEPHANT	Why can't you have a noise on the Ark.
HAM	Because the Noahs have got work to do.
FIRST ELEPHANT	Noise doesn't stop people from working.

HAM'S WIFE	Oh yes it does! It disturbs us and then we can't do our work.
SECOND ELEPHANT	What work have you got to do?
ALL ANIMALS	What have you got to do?
HAM	(*angrily*) What a question! What have we got to do? Why! We've got all the arrangements to make for you animals.
ALL ANIMALS	What arrangements?
HAM	I'll tell you! Arrangements for sleeping . . . Arrangements for washing . . .
HAM'S WIFE	Arrangements for food . . . Arrangements for . . .
FIRST ELEPHANT	(*interrupting*) Yes! Yes! I understand.
SECOND ELEPHANT	Yes, the Noahs do have a lot of work to do.
ALL ANIMALS	Yes! They do have a lot of work.
HAM	So you see that you must keep quiet and let us get on with it. Goodbye! (*He goes out.*)
HAM'S WIFE	Now look what you've done!
FIRST ELEPHANT	We didn't mean to upset him.
SECOND ELEPHANT	Elephants never mean to upset anyone.
FIRST ELEPHANT	But what shall we do?
SECOND ELEPHANT	What shall we do while the Noahs are making the arrangements?

ALL ANIMALS	Tell us? Tell us! What shall we do?
HAM'S WIFE	I know! You can have another story.
ALL ANIMALS	Yes! Yes! Another story!
HAM'S WIFE	And I know what it can be about.
ALL ANIMALS	Tell us! Tell us!
HAM'S WIFE	WORK! It can be about work. (*She goes out.*)
FIRST ELEPHANT	I know just the story. It's about a lazy camel who didn't want to work.
	Look here he comes . . .

Here begins the story of How Lazy Camel was Taught a Lesson.

How Lazy Camel was Taught a Lesson

Playmakers

CAMEL
ANTELOPE
GAZELLE

SUN BIRD
OSTRICH

LIZARD
SNAKE

GREAT TORTOISE
SPIDER
BAT

BABOON
GIRAFFE
HYENA

ROLLER BIRD
ANT

CHIEF HOWLER MONKEY who is
a magician
FIRST HOWLER MONKEY
SECOND HOWLER MONKEY

Other monkeys

How Lazy Camel was Taught a Lesson

Flat-backed CAMEL *is walking slowly along when he meets* ANTELOPE *and* GAZELLE *trotting in the opposite direction.*

ANTELOPE	Hallo Camel!
GAZELLE	You're out early!
CAMEL	Humph!
ANTELOPE	And what does 'Humph' mean, Camel?
GAZELLE	Don't you ever say anything except, 'Humph?'
CAMEL	Humph! Humph!
ANTELOPE	Look! Here come Sun Bird and Ostrich.
GAZELLE	Perhaps they will have something interesting to say.

(*Enter* SUN BIRD *and* OSTRICH.)

Good morning, Birds.

SUN BIRD	Good morning all! What a lovely, sunny day! Ah! How I love the sun on my back.
OSTRICH	Lucky you!
SUN BIRD	What do you mean, old Ostrich?
OSTRICH	The sun makes my tail feathers drop out.
SUN BIRD	Now don't start being miserable, Ostrich. It's a lovely, lovely day, isn't it, Camel?
CAMEL	Humph!
ANTELOPE	Camel doesn't think it's a lovely, lovely day.
GAZELLE	He never says anything except 'Humph!'
SUN BIRD	Never mind! Here come Lizard and Snake.

(*Enter* LIZARD *and* SNAKE.)

How does the sun suit your spiny tail, Lizard?

LIZARD	Very well! Very well!
SUN BIRD	And how does the sun suit you, Snake?
SNAKE	Ah! The sun is lovely to sleep in. I'm looking forward to a good, long sleep.
ANTELOPE	SLEEP!
GAZELLE	You can't sleep today, Snake.
SUN BIRD	You can't sleep today. We're having a meeting of the Animal Council.
CAMEL	What's that?
LIZARD	Hurrah! Camel had said something at last.
OSTRICH	What did you say, Camel?
CAMEL	I said, 'What's that?'
LIZARD	Sun Bird was saying that there is a meeting of the Animal Council.
SUN BIRD	The Animal Council is meeting here, on this spot, today, Camel.
SNAKE	So it's a very good thing that you're here.
CAMEL	Why?
SUN BIRD	WHY? Because we're meeting to discuss the animals' problems. That's why.
CAMEL	Humph!
ANTELOPE	And you have problems, haven't you, Camel?
GAZELLE	Lots of problems!
CAMEL	Humph!
SUN BIRD	It won't be any good saying 'Humph!' when Great Tortoise arrives, Camel. Great Tortoise is determined to discuss OUR GREAT PROBLEM.
CAMEL	What's that?
OSTRICH	YOU!
ALL	Sssh! Sssh!

CAMEL	What do you mean?
LIZARD	Oh well! We might as well tell him now.
SNAKE	It's you, Camel. YOU ARE THE PROBLEM.
CAMEL	ME?!
SUN BIRD	Yes! You! We're going to discuss ways of making you work.
CAMEL	WORK!?
SUN BIRD	Yes! Work! You're the laziest animal in the whole wide world and we're going to do something about it.
CAMEL	(*shuffling off*) If they're giving out jobs at this meeting, I'm off!
OSTRICH	Hi! Come back, Camel! Shall I go after him, Sun Bird?
SUN BIRD	No! He won't go far. He's much too lazy. Besides, here comes Great Tortoise, with Spider and Bat.
	(*Enter* GREAT TORTOISE, SPIDER *and* BAT.)
	Good morning, wise and honoured Chief.
ALL	Good morning, Great Tortoise.
GREAT TORTOISE	Good morning, Animal Friends. What a beautiful day for our Council meeting.
SPIDER	Come and sit here, O Wise One.
BAT	No! No! The sun will shine right into Our Wise One's eyes if he sits there.
GREAT TORTOISE	The sun doesn't worry me. In fact, I rather enjoy a little sun in my old age. But you must sit with your back to it, friend Bat, because you are used to the cool darkness of the night sky.
BAT	How kind! How kind!
SPIDER	It was good of Bat to come at all, because he's been up all night.

30

BAT	Never mind. It's in a very good cause.
GREAT TORTOISE	Ah yes! Ah yes! But we mustn't start until the others arrive.
SPIDER	I can't think why they're so late. After all, if Bat can be here on time, Baboon, Giraffe and Hyena should be here too.
BAT	I think I know why they're late. As I flew in from my night's work, I saw them clearing up a pile of thorns which Camel had left under the Kola-Kola tree.
GREAT TORTOISE	Dear me! Dear me! Were they really doing that? No doubt that pile of thorns was old Camel's bed.
LIZARD	Ssh! Someone is coming! Listen, O wise and honoured Chief!
GREAT TORTOISE	I hear no sound.
SNAKE	But we feel footsteps, Lizard and I! Being so low on the ground, we can always feel footsteps as they approach.

(*Enter* BABOON, GIRAFFE *and* HYENA *breathlessly.*)

BABOON	We ... are ... sorry ... to ... be... so ...
GIRAFFE	to ... be ... so ... late ... but ... the ... work ...
HYENA	the ... work ... left ... by ... that ... Camel!
GREAT TORTOISE	Ah yes! We have heard about your . . . er . . . good work, from our friend Bat. And we thank you for it, even if our brother Camel doesn't!
ALL	BROTHER Camel!
GREAT TORTOISE	Well, yes! Camel IS our brother. Now friends, we are meeting together today to see what can be done about Camel. Who wishes to speak?
BABOON	I do! I'm sick of clearing up after Camel.
GIRAFFE	Besides, he should do his share of the work.

31

ALL	(*loudly*) Hear! Hear!
HYENA	More than that! I think he should be punished for all his bad deeds in the past.
ALL	Punished!
HYENA	Yes! Punished! I think Camel should be punished for his past bad deeds and for his nasty, unkind ways.
SPIDER	Who's talking?!
BAT	Hyena, of course! He knows all about nasty, unkind ways because he has plenty of them himself.
GREAT TORTOISE	FRIENDS! This kind of talk won't do at all. Hyena has said that Camel has nasty, unkind ways, so now Hyena must prove it.
HYENA	I can and I will! (*shouts*) Roller Bird! Ant! Come forward!
	(ROLLER BIRD *and* ANT *limp into the Council meeting.*)
ALL	Shame! Oh, shame!
GREAT TORTOISE	Come forward, Roller Bird. You must tell us what happened to your wing. Brother Ant! Come and sit by me and tell us how you lost your poor foot. You may speak first, brother Ant.
ANT	Oh dear! I feel a little nervous in this company.
SPIDER	There is no need to feel nervous, Ant.
BAT	We are your friends.
ANT	Well . . . I don't know about that! Spiders and bats eat little ants like me.
HYENA	I didn't bring you here to make complaints about Spider and Bat, young Ant! I brought you here to tell the Council what happened in the desert this morning.

ROLLER BIRD	Let me tell the Council, because it happened to both of us.
GREAT TORTOISE	Agreed!
ALL	Agreed! Agreed!
ROLLER BIRD	Well, just as Ant was finishing his night work and beginning his day work – I'm sure you all know that Ant works all night and all day – well, just as Ant was finishing his Ant-hill home out there in the sand, ALONG CAME CAMEL.
HYENA	And what did he do, Roller? What did Camel do!
ROLLER BIRD	Camel put his great, enormous, spongy camel foot SPLODGE on Ant's home and crushed it FLAT!
GREAT TORTOISE	Very sad, I'm sure, after a night's work. But this kind of thing must often happen to Ant-hill homes. I hope you weren't inside it, brother Ant.
ANT	No! But my foot was!
ROLLER BIRD	I heard Ant crying, O Wise One. I was rolling in the sand close by, having my morning bath, so I rushed to the rescue.
HYENA	And then what did Camel do, Roller?
ROLLER BIRD	He put another of his great, enormous, spongy feet SPLODGE on my wing. He did that just as I was pulling Ant from under Camel's first foot.
ANT	And that's how I lost one of my feet. It was one of my best ones too!
GREAT TORTOISE	It's a very sad story, but I don't know whether Camel can be blamed. After all, accidents do happen.
HYENA	GO ON, Roller Bird.
ROLLER BIRD	But it wasn't an accident. Not a real accident.
GREAT TORTOISE	How do you know?

33

ANT	Because he didn't say that he was sorry.
ROLLER BIRD	He laughed!
ALL	(*horrified*) LAUGHED!
ROLLER BIRD	Yes he did! You know how Camel laughs, not properly like the rest of us, just, 'Humpph-pph-pph, humpph-pph-pph'.
HYENA	UNFORGIVABLE!
SPIDER	It sounds rather like Hyena.
BAT	Hyenas always laugh when . . .
GREAT TORTOISE	Friends! I have told you that this kind of talk won't do. Still, I have to admit that Hyena seems to have proved what he said about Camel.
HYENA	Thank you, O Wise One. So what is to be done?
ALL	What is to be done, O Wise One?
GREAT TORTOISE	CAMEL MUST BE TAUGHT A LESSON.
ALL	How?
GREAT TORTOISE	I shall have to seek advice. I shall have to go and see Howler.
ALL	(*impressed*) Howler!
GREAT TORTOISE	I shall seek advice from CHIEF HOWLER MONKEY, THE MAGICIAN. I shall go now. (*He goes.*)
HYENA	(*laughing*) Haa! Haa! Haa! I hope my animal brothers and sisters are going to thank me for the part I've played in this. Haa! Haa! Haa! Now Camel is in trouble.
SUN BIRD	Take care, Hyena, or you may be crying before nightfall. Come along, everyone. We'll all go home until Great Tortoise returns.

(*Many of the animals go out.*)

ANT	But what about me? I haven't got a home now.
SPIDER	(*laughing*) Can't you make another . . . or would you like to come with me, Ant?
BAT	Or me?
SUN BIRD	Stop teasing poor Ant. Come with me Ant. You shall have a nice safe place in my nest until Great Tortoise returns. (*They go out.*)

(*Several animals enter carrying trees in pots, which they position in arena to represent forest, then go out again.* GREAT TORTOISE *lumbers in.*)

GREAT TORTOISE	What a strange and shadowy place this is! I'm glad I don't live near the forest. Tortoises just don't like trees. Let's hope Chief Howler Monkey is at home. (*shouting*) HOWLER! HOWLER! HOWLER!
CHIEF HOWLER	(*from off stage*) Who calls?
GREAT TORTOISE	It's Great Tortoise.
CHIEF HOWLER	(*from off stage*) Stay there, O Wise One. I'm coming.

(*Enter* CHIEF HOWLER MONKEY.)

What brings you to my Howley-Howley home at the edge of the forest, O Wise One?

GREAT TORTOISE	I've got a problem. Indeed, brother Howler, ALL the animals have a problem.
CHIEF HOWLER	Is it the same problem?
GREAT TORTOISE	It is! It's Camel!
CHIEF HOWLER	Oh him! What's old Humph done now?
GREAT TORTOISE	That's the point. He won't do anything. He's lazy, untidy and, worst of all, UNKIND. What can we do about him?

CHIEF HOWLER	Cut his rations! Those who won't work shouldn't eat.
GREAT TORTOISE	We can't do that. We don't live in family groups like you monkeys. Besides, he eats things the rest of us don't like.
CHIEF HOWLER	Like what?
GREAT TORTOISE	Like the prickles of the Prickle-Stickle Tree . . . and the thorns of the Spiker-Piker Bush . . . and the spines of the Pin-Cushion Cactus . . . and things like that.
CHIEF HOWLER	Does he really enjoy his food?
GREAT TORTOISE	Oh yes! Perhaps it's eating so many prickly, spiky things that makes him so grumpy and lazy. What I really want to do, Howler, is to change his heart.
CHIEF HOWLER	So you want to change his heart, O Wise One! Well, you send him to me and I'll change him all right. I'll begin by changing the shape of him.
GREAT TORTOISE	What do you mean?
CHIEF HOWLER	You just leave that to me and my Monkey Magic. Just send him along here.
GREAT TORTOISE	But how can I get him to come?
CHIEF HOWLER	Just tell him . . . just tell him . . . that Chief Howler Monkey has got a huge stack of . . . Delicious Desert Delights. Just tell him that.
GREAT TORTOISE	What are Delicious Desert Delights?
CHIEF HOWLER	SCRUMPTIOUS! . . . Ah! We won't tell him what they are. You just tell him to come for EXTRA RATIONS.
GREAT TORTOISE	But suppose he won't come!

36

CHIEF HOWLER	He will! That old Camel is very curious and very greedy.
GREAT TORTOISE	Well, it's worth a try. I'll go and talk to the other animals about it. (*He goes out.*)
CHIEF HOWLER	(*calls*) Howler-Howler-Howler-Howler- HOW-W-W-W-W-L-E-R! Howler-Howler-Howler-Howler- HOW-W-W-W-W-L-E-R!

(*Enter group of* HOWLER MONKEYS.)

ALL HOWLERS	You-Called-You-Called-You-Called- Y-O-U-C-A—L-L-E-D!
CHIEF HOWLER	Bring me a bag made from the leaves of the Prickle-Stickle Tree.

(FIRST HOWLER *goes out.*)
Now we must make Monkey Magic.

ALL HOWLERS	Whoo-for-whoo-for-whoo-for-whoo-for?
CHIEF HOWLER	For Camel who loves his food, but will not work.

(*Enter* FIRST HOWLER.)

FIRST HOWLER	Here is the bag made from the leaves of the Prickle-Stickle Tree, O Chief.
CHIEF HOWLER	Camel likes all prickly-stickly things. Fetch! Fetch! Fetch!

(*Several* HOWLERS *go out.*)

Camel likes all spiny-twiny things.
Fetch! Fetch! Fetch!

(*Several* HOWLERS *go out.*)

Camel likes all horny-thorny things.
Fetch! Fetch! Fetch!

(*Several* HOWLERS *go out.*)

CHIEF HOWLER *cont*	Now hold open the top of the bag made from the leaves of the Prickle-Stickle Tree.
SECOND HOWLER	Yes, Great Chief.
	(*Enter* MONKEYS, *carrying twigs, spiky branches, etc.*)
ALL HOWLERS	(*chanting as they put materials into bag*) Prickly-stickly-Camel-trouble, In the bag to hubble-stubble!
	Spiny-twiny-Camel-trouble. In the bag to hubble-stubble!
	Horny-thorny-Camel-trouble, In the bag to hubble-stubble!
	(*Enter* GREAT TORTOISE.)
GREAT TORTOISE	Howler! Howler! Are you there? CAMEL IS COMING!
CHIEF HOWLER	Take the Monkey Magic away!
	(HOWLERS *go out.*)
	Stay in the shadows, O Wise One, where Camel cannot see you.
	(*Enter* CAMEL.)
	Ah! If it isn't my old friend Camel! What a surprise! What brings you to my Howley-Howley home on the edge of the forest, brother Camel?
CAMEL	Where is it?
CHIEF HOWLER	Where's what?
CAMEL	Humph! This FOOD.
CHIEF HOWLER	Oh! you mean that you want some Monkey Magic. You'd like a taste of our Delicious Desert Delights, would you?
CAMEL	Humph! Humph! What are they made of?
CHIEF HOWLER	You'll see! You'll see!
CAMEL	Humph! I can't see anything.

CHIEF HOWLER	You are impatient, aren't you Camel? Perhaps they're not quite ready yet. My monkey brothers are just finishing them over there, behind the trees. (*He points off stage.*)
CAMEL	Humph! (*walking in the direction pointed*) I'll take a look. (*He goes out.*)
CHIEF HOWLER	(*to* GREAT TORTOISE) Come over here and I'll whisper. (*He makes a very long stage whisper to* GREAT TORTOISE, *who looks more and more amazed, then begins to laugh.*)
	Now to Monkey Magic!
GREAT TORTOISE	(*laughing*) I can't . . . I can't . . . I can't believe it. A . . . permanent pantry . . . on his back! (*He falls over in helpless laughter.*) Permanent pantry! Permanent pantry!
	(*Enter all animals who attended Council meeting, led by* SUN BIRD.)
	Per-man-ent PAN-try! (*He lies back exhausted from laughing.*)
SUN BIRD	What can have happened to our wise and honoured Chief? Why does he say these strange words? He must be ill.
SPIDER	Speak to us, Great Tortoise.
BAT	What a good thing we followed him.
SUN BIRD	I know! I'll make a cool breeze with my wings.
GREAT TORTOISE	(*sitting up*) Well! Well! Well!
ALL ANIMALS	(*showing relief*) He's better! He's better!
GREAT TORTOISE	I wasn't ill, my friends. I was just laughing!
ALL ANIMALS	Laughing!
GREAT TORTOISE	When you see our brotner Camel, you will all laugh too. Chief Howler Monkey has made great monkey magic – a kind of MONKEY TRICK. He is at this moment, changing Camel's shape PERMANENTLY!

SUN BIRD	Permanently! What is going on? When we found you, Great Tortoise, you were lying there saying, 'permanent pantry', over and over again.
GREAT TORTOISE	A PERMANENT PANTRY! That's what our brother Camel is going to have on his back. When I explained our problem to Chief Howler Monkey . . .
SUN BIRD	When you told him that Camel wouldn't work for days and days . . .
GREAT TORTOISE	Chief Howler said . . . 'Then we must make him so that he doesn't eat for days and days and days'.
ALL ANIMALS	But Camel will . . . DIE!
GREAT TORTOISE	Die! Oh no! He'll just live off this permanent pantry, which he will carry around on his back for the rest of his life. LOOK!
	(*Enter* CHIEF HOWLER MONKEY, *leading humped* CAMEL, *with other* HOWLERS *behind.*)
CHIEF HOWLER	Here he is! Here's brother Camel in his new shape.
ALL ANIMALS	Look! Look at Camel's . . .
SUN BIRD	Permanent pantry!
HYENA	You'll be able to work for days and days and days now, Camel, without eating at all.
CAMEL	Humph! Humph! Humph! How can I work with this big lump on my back?
HYENA	Not lump, Camel! HUMPH!
SUN BIRD	Not Humph! HUMP!
ALL ANIMALS	Hump! Camel's got a HUMP!
	(CAMEL *staggers off slowly.*)
ALL ANIMALS	(*following*) Hump! Hump! Camel's got a hump!
SUN BIRD	And he's got a permanent pantry too!

40

ALL ANIMALS (*sing as they go off, to the 'All Aboard' tune:*)

So Camel's humph became a lump,
Humph and humph and humph!
And now his pantry's in his HUMP!
Humph and humph and humph!

(*Chorus from off stage*)

Humph and humph,
Old Camel's got a hump!
Humph and humph,
Old Camel's got a hump!

END OF SECOND PLAY

PLAYWATCHERS

All Aboard

Applause from 'All Aboard' animals

FIRST GIRAFFE I wish I had a permanent pantry on my back.

SECOND GIRAFFE But you'd look so ugly, my dear. I like you just as you are!

FIRST GIRAFFE But I'm hungry.

SECOND GIRAFFE Yes! I'm hungry too.

ALL ANIMALS We're all hungry! We want food! FOOD! FOOD! WE WANT F O O D! (*general uproar*)

(*Enter* SHEM *and* WIFE.)

SHEM Stop! Stop! You're making a terrible noise. STOP!

(*Animals quieten down*)

SHEM'S WIFE We can't have a noise like that on the Ark.

FIRST GIRAFFE Why not?

SHEM You know why not! You know it's because we've got work to do. You know that the Noahs are making arrangements for you animals.

SECOND GIRAFFE We're hungry. We want food!

ALL ANIMALS WE WANT FOOD!

SHEM As I was saying, we're making all the arrangements for you animals and they include food.

FIRST GIRAFFE	Well, I wish you'd hurry up with your arrangements about the food because we're hungry.
SECOND GIRAFFE	We want food, NOT arrangements!
ALL ANIMALS	WE WANT FOOD! WE WANT FOOD!
SHEM	Don't be so impatient! We've prepared the food. Now we have to share it out. (*He goes out.*)
SHEM'S WIFE	Each of you must have a fair share.
FIRST GIRAFFE	If you've prepared the food, then let's have it.
SECOND GIRAFFE	Just bring it in and we'll share it out.
SHEM'S WIFE	We can't do that. Some of you animals are unfair to each other.
ALL ANIMALS	(*looking at each other*) US?
SHEM'S WIFE	Yes! You! Some of you big strong ones are very unfair to the smaller weak ones. You're unfair and unkind. Do you remember the story of The Great Tug of War?
ALL ANIMALS	No! Tell us! Tell us!
SHEM'S WIFE	Look. Here comes a group of these poor little creatures! You can see for yourselves what I mean!

Here begins the story of The Great Tug of War.

The Great Tug of War

Playmakers

RABBIT
SQUIRREL
HARE

FIRST DORMOUSE
SECOND DORMOUSE
THIRD DORMOUSE

BOMBO THE ELEPHANT

FROG
TOAD

DIPPER
FLY CATCHER
SPARROW
FIRST BELL BIRD
SECOND BELL BIRD
FIRST WARBLER
SECOND WARBLER

HIPPO THE HIPPOPOTAMUS

BUZZ THE MOSQUITO
SQUEEZY THE ROCK PYTHON

The Great Tug of War

RABBIT, SQUIRREL *and* HARE *come in, shaking themselves.*

RABBIT   Oh, my fur and whiskers! (*brushing fur with paws*) Just look at me! I'm soaking wet!

SQUIRREL   (*shaking tail*) Look at my poor tail! It's ruined!

HARE   (*patting ears with paws*) My ears! My ears! I can't hear properly! I think I'm going deaf.

RABBIT   (*turning round and patting tail*) How would that Elephant like having a damp cushion to sit on?

SQUIRREL   Or a wet scarf hanging round his neck?

HARE   (*shaking ears*) Or ears full of water? A-tish-oo! I've got a terrible cold in the head already. A-tish-oo!

ALL THREE   A-tish-oo! A-tish-oo! A-tish-oo!

RABBIT   There! Now we've all caught a cold because of Elephant.

SQUIRREL   Old Bombo just doesn't care.

HARE   He comes barging along every morning, knocking everyone over. And now this!

RABBIT   His trunk must have been FULL of water.

SQUIRREL   Why can't he shower it over his own great fat body? There's enough of it!

HARE   A-tish-oo (*springing into air*) A-tish-oo! A-tish-oo! Whatever's that?

(*All listen . . . Sounds of screeching and squeaking.*)

I heard something! I heard something! Oh dear! My nerves are in a terrible state!

RABBIT	Listen!
	(*Louder sounds of screeching and squeaking.*)
	Well at least it's not Elephant! Old Bombo sounds like thunder when he trumpets along.
	(*Enter small family of* DORMICE, *screeching and squeaking and running round in circles.*)
SQUIRREL	Whatever's the matter with you Dormice?
HARE	Stop running round in circles! Stop! STOP! You'll make yourselves dizzy.
	(RABBIT, SQUIRREL *and* HARE *hold onto* DORMICE *and pat them gently.*)
FIRST DORMOUSE	It's terrible! It's terrible!
SECOND DORMOUSE	It's ruined! It's ruined!
THIRD DORMOUSE	There's nothing left! Nothing at all!
RABBIT	What's terrible? What's ruined?
SQUIRREL	Have you been robbed?
HARE	Has someone broken into your home?
ALL DORMICE	(*wailing loudly*) Home! HOME!
FIRST DORMOUSE	Don't say HOME.
SECOND DORMOUSE	You must never say, HOME, to us again.
THIRD DORMOUSE	We're homeless!
ALL DORMICE	HOMELESS!
RABBIT, HARE, SQUIRREL	How?
ALL DORMICE	It's Bombo! (*They sob wildly.*) Bombo! Bombo!
RABBIT	(*kindly*) Come along! Pull yourselves together! What has Bombo done now?
FIRST DORMOUSE	He came barging along . . .
SECOND DORMOUSE	. . . on his great, enormous feet . . .

THIRD DORMOUSE	. . . and flattened our home! There's nothing left! There's nothing left at all!
SQUIRREL	There must be something left. I know Bombo's got big feet, but . . .
ALL DORMICE	(*shaking heads*) THERE'S NOTHING LEFT!
FIRST DORMOUSE	There's nothing left of our home.
SECOND DORMOUSE	And if we'd been in it, there'd be nothing left of us either!
THIRD DORMOUSE	Because he trod on it, then he turned himself round on it, then he trampled on it, and then he sat on it!
FIRST DORMOUSE	He's there now.
SECOND DORMOUSE	He's having his morning sleep.
THIRD DORMOUSE	ON OUR HOME!
RABBIT	(*firmly*) Something will have to be done!
SQUIRREL	Bombo will have to be stopped.
HARE	Agreed! Bombo will have to be stopped.
	(BOMBO *lumbers in.*)
BOMBO	Hello! Hello! Did I hear someone telling me to stop? Well . . . (*standing still*) . . . I have!
RABBIT	(*angrily*) Bombo! You know you heard us saying that you would have TO BE STOPPED!
BOMBO	Same thing!
RABBIT	No, it isn't.
BOMBO	Don't argue with me, Puff Tail! I've saved you a lot of trouble by stopping all on my own. It just shows what a nice, kind Elephant I am.
ALL ANIMALS	Nice! Kind! (*pointing at Bombo*) YOU!
BOMBO	(*happily*) Yes! Me!

RABBIT	Now, listen to me, Bombo. We don't think you're nice and kind. In fact we were just deciding what to do to stop you from being so . . .
SQUIRREL	HORRIBLE!
HARE	Yes! Horrible!
BOMBO	(*in astonishment*) Me! Horrible! What a nerve! Oh well, I can't please everybody in this world, so I may as well not bother any more.
ALL ANIMALS	(*angrily*) ANY MORE!
RABBIT	You have never cared about anybody except yourself, Bombo. So just you listen to us . . .

(*All* ANIMALS *bar Bombo's path.*)

BOMBO	So you little whipper-snappers want me to listen to you, do you? All right! I'm listening!
RABBIT	(*firmly*) You've got to stop . . . BARGING ABOUT.
SQUIRREL	(*firmly*) You've got to stop . . . HOSING US DOWN.
HARE	(*firmly*) You've got to stop . . . CRUSHING PEOPLE'S HOMES.
ALL ANIMALS	Or else . . . or else . . .
BOMBO	Or else WHAT?
RABBIT	Or . . . we'll do something about it!
BOMBO	(*laughing*) Ho-Ho-Ho! So you'll do something about it! Like what may I ask?
RABBIT	LIKE . . . Well . . . We don't know yet.
BOMBO	(*laughing*) Ho-Ho-Ho! So you don't know yet! Oh well, let me know when you do know.

(BOMBO *begins to push the animals to one side.*)

ALL ANIMALS	Stop! STOP! S T O P!

48

BOMBO	Ho-Ho-Ho! Do your worst, Scream and shout until you burst! I'm off!
	(BOMBO *pushes his way through the animals. They follow him, crying, 'Stop! Stop!' *FROG *and* TOAD *come in from the same side.*)
FROG	(*looking back*) Whatever was all that about?
TOAD	Bombo's made trouble again, I suppose! Of course, he doesn't make any difference to us.
FROG	No, but Hippo does! Do you know, Toad, when I was sitting on my lily pad this morning, waiting to catch some flies for breakfast, there was a great big SWOOSH . . .
TOAD	Don't tell me! Let me guess . . . Hippo!
FROG	Yes! Hippo! Taking his morning bath!
TOAD	So you had a mud bath too, I suppose.
FROG	Yes! And no breakfast! It's too bad.
TOAD	Hippo's a great, big bully.
FROG	These heavy-weights are all the same. And they have no idea at all of the trouble they cause.
TOAD	Trouble? Listen! (*noisy twittering of* BIRDS) That sounds like trouble! It's the birds this time.
	(BIRDS *swoop in, twittering and chattering.*)
FROG	(*enquiringly*) What's the matter? Was it Bombo?
TOAD	Or was it Hippo?
ALL BIRDS	(*swooping round in great distress*) Bombo AND Hippo! Bombo AND Hippo!
FROG	My goodness! You Bell Birds and Warblers do make a noise! Calm down! Calm down!
TOAD	(*soothingly*) Come and perch over here, Fly Catcher . . . and you, Sparrow.

49

FROG	Well, Dipper! We can see who you've met this morning. You're covered in mud.
DIPPER	It was Hippo! When my wings are covered in mud like this, I can't fly properly. It's too bad! (*He shakes himself.*)
FROG	Never mind! You can soon dip down into the river and wash it away, so do stop fussing.
DIPPER	I can't wash it away! Hippo has churned up the mud in the river so that it's like thick brown treacle.
FLY CATCHER	He did it on purpose. We saw him.
SPARROW	He does it every morning, so we birds can't have a bath. And it's gone into my nest!
FIRST BELL BIRD	What about our nest? It's full of water. It's flooded out!
SECOND BELL BIRD	Bombo did it.
FIRST WARBLER	Bombo's as bad as Hippo.
SECOND WARBLER	Bombo's worse than Hippo. This morning he shook us out of our nest.
FROG	Listen! (*thundering footsteps*)
TOAD	Here comes TROUBLE!
FROG	Is it Bombo?
TOAD	Or is it Hippo?
	(HIPPO *lumbers slowly in.*)
ALL	HIPPO!
HIPPO	(*slowly*) Did somebody speak? Good morning!
FROG	Ah! But it isn't a good morning for some of us, is it Hippo?
HIPPO	(*slowly*) The morning looks all right to me.

50

TOAD	That's because you're looking at it from your point of view, Hippo. That's the trouble with you heavy-weights. You're selfish!
HIPPO	Well, you don't expect me to look at it from the point of view of some miserable little toad, do you?
TOAD	(*furiously*) How dare you?
FROG	Now, look here, Hippo. It's time you started having a bit of consideration for others. Just look at these birds.
HIPPO	Birds! Birds! What about them?
FROG	Some of them are covered in mud. YOUR MUD! It's the mud you churned up this morning when you were having your bath.
HIPPO	Oh, I see! The birds got a free bath! Oh well . . . I just hope they're grateful to me, that's all.
ALL BIRDS	(*angrily*) Grateful! GRATEFUL!
HIPPO	Mud baths are good for people, and this one was free! It was FREE! (*laughing*) Haw-Haw-Haw! Say thank you to Hippo! Haw-Haw-Haw! (*He begins to lumber out, then calls back.*) Another mud bath's going free! You're all welcome . . . half past three! Haw-Haw-Haw!
	(*As HIPPO lumbers out, RABBIT, SQUIRREL and HARE, with the DORMICE, pass him on their way back in.*)
ALL BIRDS	(*furiously*) Do something about him! Do something about him!
RABBIT	Do something about who?
ALL BIRDS	(*swooping and twittering round animals*) Hippo! Hippo! Hippo!
SQUIRREL	What's Hippo done?

HARE	He was laughing!
DIPPER	He was laughing at me. Look! I'm covered with mud from his mud bath this morning.
FIRST DORMOUSE	He was saying a rhyme as he went by. He was saying . . .
ALL DORMICE	'Another mud bath going free! You're all welcome . . . half past three!'
TOAD	And he was rude to me. He called me a . . . miserable . . . little . . . TOAD!
ALL	(*in horror*) OooooooH!
FROG	The time has come! Something MUST be done about Hippo.
ALL DORMICE	And Bombo!
ALL	Hippo and Bombo!
TOAD	But what? What can we do?
RABBIT	And who can do it? That's the problem.
SQUIRREL	None of us is strong enough alone.
HARE	Then we must do something together.
ALL	WHAT? (*They sit and look at each other gloomily.*)
HARE	(*springing into air*) I know!
ALL	(*eagerly*) What?
HARE	I don't know what . . . yet. But I know who to ask.
ALL	(*eagerly*) Who?
HARE	Squeezy and Buzz!
ALL	(*in surprise*) Squeezy and Buzz!
FROG	(*thoughtfully*) Everyone is afraid of Squeezy and Buzz, but what could they actually DO to Hippo and Bombo?
TOAD	Let's ask them. Now . . . who's quickest at flying?

SPARROW	Me!
FLY CATCHER	And me! We'll both go. Come on, Sparrow! (*They swoop out.*)
FIRST BELL BIRD	(*nervously*) Aren't they brave?
SECOND BELL BIRD	They say that Squeezy eats birds.
FIRST WARBLER	(*pointing*) And frogs and toads.
SECOND WARBLER	(*pointing*) And all members of your family, Rabbit.
RABBIT	He won't hurt us. Squeezy's our friend.
SQUIRREL	And Buzz is Squeezy's friend, so we're all right.
HARE	Buzz only hurts humans, anyway. You should see humans run and get under their nets when they hear Buzz coming!
FROG	(*hearing faint buzzing sound*) Listen! That's the buzz of a . . . mosquito. (*hearing a faint hissing sound*) Listen! That's the hiss of a . . . Rock Python.
	(BUZZ *comes in with jerky, darting movements, followed by* SQUEEZY *with* SPARROW *and* FLY CATCHER.)
SQUEEZY	Well! (*settling down*) So you've got a bit of trouble
BUZZ	. . . with Bombo and Hippo!
ALL	Do something! Do something!
SQUEEZY	Easier said than done! It's a long way round Bombo's body.
BUZZ	And I can't get my sting through Hippo's thick skin.
ALL	DO SOMETHING!
SQUEEZY	There's only one way. (*He hisses to* BUZZ.)
BUZZ	(*nodding*) I agree. (*He buzzes to* SQUEEZY, *who nods.*)

53

ALL	WHAT?
SQUEEZY	Make 'em fight each other!
BUZZ	At least make them use their strength against each other.
ALL	HOW?
SQUEEZY	Simple! Tug of War!
BUZZ	That's it! A Tug of War against EACH OTHER!
	(*All listeners cheer and clap.*)
HARE	(*springing into air*) That's it! That's it! We'll have Squeezy to be the rope.
SQUEEZY	(*looking annoyed*) Do you mind! I'm not a bit of elastic.
BUZZ	What a silly idea!
	(HARE *hides behind others.*)
	You birds must make a strong rope with creepers and vines. Weave them together so that you've got the thickest and strongest rope in the world. Go on . . . Off you go!
ALL BIRDS	We will! We will! (*They swoop out.*)
RABBIT	But will Bombo and Hippo agree to have a Tug of War against each other?
SQUEEZY	Agree! We're not going to tell 'em.
BUZZ	They won't know they're pulling EACH OTHER.
SQUEEZY	We'll tie 'em up so they can't see each other.
BUZZ	(*patiently*) The idea is that one of you challenges Bombo to the Tug of War, and another of you challenges Hippo.
SQUEEZY	Rabbit can challenge Bombo and Sparrow can challenge Hippo.
BUZZ	That's settled then.

SQUEEZY	Fetch 'em in . . . one at a time . . . Bombo first.
HARE	(*springing up*) I'll go! I'll go! (*He runs out.*)
RABBIT	What have I got to say when Bombo comes?
BUZZ	Leave it to us. It will be quite easy. You'll see!

(BOMBO *lumbers slowly in, followed by* HARE.)

HARE	I told him you'd thought of something to do to him, Rabbit.
SQUEEZY	Tell that silly Hare to get lost!

(HARE, *looking foolish, hides behind others again.*)

Now, Bombo! I hear you've been throwing your weight about again.

BOMBO	Ho-Ho-Ho! Me! You know what these little whipper-snappers are like, Squeezy.
BUZZ	Whipper-snappers! I don't know about that. This Rabbit's a very strong fellow.
BOMBO	Rabbit! Strong! Ho-Ho-Ho!
RABBIT	I'm a very strong fellow . . . and I challenge you . . . Bombo . . . to a Tug of War.
BOMBO	A WHAT?
RABBIT	A TUG OF WAR.
BOMBO	Just you?
RABBIT	Just me!
BOMBO	Ho-Ho-Ho! Did you hear that, Squeezy?
SQUEEZY	I heard all right. What about it?
BOMBO	You can't be serious, Rabbit?
BUZZ	Are you serious, Rabbit?
RABBIT	Very serious.
BOMBO	(*nastily*) Where's the . . . bit of string?

BUZZ	The birds are making a thick, strong rope. They'll be back in a minute.
BOMBO	Ho-Ho-Ho! Perhaps I'd better go and have a sleep to get my strength up. Wake me when you're ready! Ho-Ho-Ho! (*He lumbers out laughing.*)
SQUEEZY	Fetch Hippo!
HARE	(*springing up*) I'll go! I'll go!
SQUIRREL	No! You'd better stay here with us.
RABBIT	And help me to get my strength up! (*laughing*) He-He-He!
FROG	I'll go, because I know just where he is.
TOAD	I'll come with you Frog. After all, he was so rude to me. I want to see him put down. (*They go out.*)
BUZZ	I hope the birds are getting on with the rope.
SQUEEZY	Go and hurry 'em up, Buzz. And send Sparrow back here.
	(BUZZ *darts out.* HIPPO *lumbers in, followed by* FROG *and* TOAD.)
HIPPO	Now what's all this about, Squeezy? I was just having a nice snooze when these two little reptiles came and woke me up.
FROG and TOAD	Reptiles! Anyone knows we're not reptiles!
SQUEEZY	Now, Hippo! I hear you've been throwing your weight about again.
HIPPO	Me! (*laughing*) Haw-Haw-Haw! So these little reptiles have been complaining about their free mud baths, have they? Haw-Haw-Haw! They were free, you know!
	(SPARROW *comes in, followed by* BUZZ.)
BUZZ	(*to* SQUEEZY) Sparrow knows all about it. (*to* HIPPO) Sparrow's got something to say to you, Hippo. Go on, Sparrow!

SPARROW   (*nervously*) Please Hippo . . .

BUZZ   No! Not like that Sparrow. (*whispering*) You've got to sound big and strong.

HIPPO   What's the matter, Sparrow? Do you want a free mud bath?

SPARROW   (*angrily*) No, I don't! I challenge you, Hippo, to a Tug of War!

HIPPO   A WHAT?

SPARROW   A TUG OF WAR.

HIPPO   Just you?

SPARROW   Just me.

HIPPO   You can't be serious!

SPARROW   Yes, I am. The other birds are making a big strong rope for us to pull with.

BUZZ   Look! They're bringing it in now.

(BIRDS *come in, carrying the rope which they tie round* HIPPO'S *body.*)

SQUEEZY   I hope you're quite happy about this, Hippo?

HIPPO   Haw-Haw-Haw! Can't you see? I'm frightened to death! Haw-Haw-Haw! When are we going to start?

BUZZ   In a minute. But you'd better go and finish your snooze first.

HIPPO   All right! Wake me up when you're ready. No! On second thoughts, don't bother! I could pull all this lot fast asleep. (*He lumbers out, laughing, leaving the end of the rope with the animals.*)

BUZZ   Now, take this end and get Bombo tied up.

BUZZ   Come on, Birds. Bring the rope.

(BUZZ *and* BIRDS *take the end of the rope out on Bombo's side.*)

HARE	Is there anything we can do, Squeezy?
SQUEEZY	Tie a ribbon to the middle of the rope.
	(RABBIT, SQUIRREL *and* HARE *tie a ribbon on the middle of rope.*)
FROG	Is there anything we can do, Squeezy?
SQUEEZY	Nothing at all . . . except enjoy yourselves!
	(BUZZ *and* BIRDS *come back.*)
BUZZ	Here we are! Bombo's ready! Now we'll give Hippo a tug on the rope to wake him up. (*He tugs the rope.*)
SQUEEZY	Give Bombo a shout, everybody!
ALL	(*call*) Bombo! Ready!
SQUEEZY	Give Hippo a shout everybody!
ALL	(*call*) Hippo! Ready!
	(*The rope is slowly tightened across the arena.*)
BUZZ	(*calls*) Are you ready? . . . PULL!
	(*Ribbon travels to left, then to right, and animals follow with head movements.*)
ALL	(*call to Bombo*) Pull, Bombo! Pull harder! (*call to Hippo*) Pull, Hippo! Pull harder!
	(*Loud thuds and groans from both sides. Rope slackens.*)
VOICE OF BOMBO	Who pulled that time?
RABBIT	(*calls*) Me! Rabbit! Puff Tail!
VOICE OF BOMBO	Mighty big Rabbit!
RABBIT	Can't you pull a little whipper-snapper like me, Bombo? (*to others*) He-He-He!
VOICE OF BOMBO	Of course I can! I was just having a rest, that's all.
	(*All listeners roll about in silent pleasure.*)
BUZZ	(*calls*) Are you ready for another pull, Hippo?

VOICE OF HIPPO	Who pulled last time?
SPARROW	(*calls*) Me! Sparrow!
VOICE OF HIPPO	Mighty strong Sparrow!
SPARROW	(*calls*) Can't you pull a poor little thing like me, Hippo?
VOICE OF HIPPO	Of course I can! I was just having a rest, that's all.
	(*All listeners roll about in silent pleasure.*)
BUZZ	(*calls*) It's time for the next pull. Are you ready? . . . PULL!
	(*The rope is tightened across the arena. Ribbon travels to left, then to right, and animals follow with head movements.*)
ALL	(*call to Bombo*) Pull, Bombo! Pull harder!
HARE	(*springing into air with excitement*) Pull, Jelly Baby! Pull, Jelly Baby!
ALL	(*call to Hippo*) Pull, Hippo! Pull, harder!
DIPPER	(*swooping about with excitement*) Pull, Jelly Fish! Pull, Jelly Fish!
	(*Loud thuds and groans from both sides. Rope slackens.*)
BUZZ	(*calls*) Get up and pull, Bombo!
HARE	(*calls*) You great, fat Jelly Baby!
ALL	(*call*) Go on, Bombo, Do your worst! Tug and pull until you burst!
BUZZ	(*calls*) Get up and pull, Hippo!
DIPPER	(*calls*) You great, fat Jelly Fish!
ALL	(*call*) Go on, Hippo, Do your worst! Tug and pull until you burst!

(*Rope tightens across arena.*)

ALL   (*call to Bombo*) Pull harder!

(*call to Hippo*) Pull harder!

(SQUEEZY *squirms forward with scissors, which he holds up for everyone to see.*)

Pull! Pull! Pull! Pull!

(SQUEEZY *cuts rope. Loud thuds and groans from both sides. All roll about with pleasure.*)

(*shout*) NOW WHO'S A WHIPPER-SNAPPER? WHO'S A REPTILE NOW?
Jelly Baby! Jelly Baby!
Jelly Fish! Jelly Fish!

SQUEEZY   (*shouts*) Fetch 'em here!

(SQUIRREL, RABBIT *and* HARE *rush to Bombo's side.* FROG, TOAD *and* DORMICE *rush to Hippo's side.*)

BUZZ   Now perhaps they'll listen to reason.

(BOMBO *and* HIPPO *are pulled into view, moaning and groaning.*)

BOMBO   Oww! Oww! My poor head!

HIPPO   Oww! Oww! My poor back!

BOMBO, HIPPO   Oww! Oww! OWW! OWW!

SQUEEZY   Stop that horrible noise!

BOMBO   You don't know what it's like, Squeezy. I've got the most terrible bump on my head.

HIPPO   I'm bruised all over.

SQUEEZY   Now you two heavy-weights know what it's like to be battered and bruised. Perhaps, in future, you'll have a little more consideration (*pointing*) for these poor little animals.

BUZZ   Well! Will you?

ALL	WILL YOU?
BOMBO, HIPPO	YES! YES! WE WILL!
ALL	PROMISE?
BOMBO, HIPPO	WE PROMISE! WE PROMISE!
SQUEEZY	Then get off home and behave yourselves.
BOMBO	I can't! I can't get up!
HIPPO	Nor me! I'm in agony!
BUZZ	(*darting forward with a very large syringe*) All right, then! I'll give you one of my injections!
BOMBO, HIPPO	No! NO! N O!

(BOMBO *and* HIPPO *struggle to their feet and blunder off, to wild cheers of all.*)

ALL (*sing to the 'All Aboard' tune:*)

That served them right – what do you say?
Heave and ho and heave!
They *did* feel sore for many a day!
Heave and ho and heave!

E N D   O F   T H I R D   P L A Y

61

PLAYWATCHERS

All Aboard

Applause from 'All Aboard' animals who mime Tug of War with each other, then fall about as they take up the refrain.

> *Chorus*
> Heave and ho,
> Aboard the floating Zoo.
> Heave and ho,
> Aboard the floating Zoo.
>
> (*There is general uproar as* HAM *and* WIFE *come in. They try to quieten the animals.*)

HAM	What a dreadful noise!
HAM'S WIFE	Stop! Stop at once!

(*Noise continues with singing etc. Enter* SHEM *and* WIFE.)

SHEM	What a terrible noise!
SHEM'S WIFE	Stop! Stop at once!

(*Noise continues. Enter* JAPHET *and* WIFE.)

JAPHET	What a ghastly noise!
JAPHET'S WIFE	Stop! Stop at once!

(*Noise continues. Enter* NOAH.)

NOAH	(*shouts*) Mrs Noah can't stand it any longer! I tell you she can't stand it any longer! (*Noise quietens a little.*) She can't stand it! It's sending her crazy! It's making her . . . (*puts head in hands*)

(HAM, SHEM *and* JAPHET *rush over to him.*)

HAM	What is it?
NOAH	What do you think it is? . . . She's going out of her mind!
SHEM	What shall we do?
NOAH	Oh, my poor wife! My poor old dear! Well . . . it just can't go on.
JAPHET	Tell us what to do, father.

(NOAH *whispers to* HAM, *who whispers to* SHEM, *who whispers to* JAPHET. *Noise increases during whispering.*)

NOAH	Come with me, Ham. (*They go out. Noise decreases then increases.*)
SHEM	It's getting worse again.
JAPHET	It's getting worse every minute. (*noise increases*)
WIVES	What is?
SHEM	Shall we tell them?
JAPHET	I think we'd better.

(SHEM *whispers to* HAM'S WIFE, *who whispers to* SHEM'S WIFE *who whispers to* JAPHET'S WIFE.)

ALL WIVES	(*scream*) Aah! AAh! AAH! (*sudden quiet*)
FIRST ELEPHANT	Whatever is the matter?
ALL WIVES	Aah! AAh! AAH!
FIRST ELEPHANT	Can't you stop them from making so much noise?

ALL WIVES	Aah! AAh! AAH!
FIRST GIRAFFE	What's wrong?
SHEM	I dread to think!
JAPHET	You may well ask!
FIRST GIRAFFE	Well, we do ask.
SHEM	It's a CALAMITY!
JAPHET	It's a DISASTER!
ALL ANIMALS	WHAT IS?
SHEM	This TERRIBLE MISFORTUNE.
ALL ANIMALS	What MISFORTUNE?
JAPHET	The worst misfortune that could possibly happen.
ALL ANIMALS	Tell us!
SHEM	(*to* JAPHET) Do you think we should?
JAPHET	Well . . . (*He whispers to* SHEM *who nods.*) All animals on board the Ark must prepare themselves for . . . Well, go on . . . PREPARE YOURSELVES!
	(*All animals silent. Many put paws together. Some look fearful.*)
SHEM	I'll begin at this end with Elephant. When I've told him. He must PASS IT ON. Are you ready, Elephant? IT'S . . . (*whispers*)

(FIRST ELEPHANT *whispers to* SECOND ELEPHANT *and says, 'pass it on,' when he has finished. This continues along row and along other rows until all animals have been told.*)

JAPHET (*to last animal*) You'd better stand up and tell us what you heard. We must be certain that you got the right message.

LAST ANIMAL I . . . I . . . I . . .

SHEM Go on!

LAST ANIMAL I . . . can't say it.

JAPHET GO ON! SAY IT!

LAST ANIMAL It's . . . CONSTANTDRIPPING!

ALL ANIMALS CONSTANTDRIPPING! (*All cower, heads on front legs/paws. Some peep fearfully. Silence is broken as* MRS NOAH *enters with a flourish.*)

MRS NOAH There! I told you it would work! (*to animals*) Well now, my dear animals. CAN YOU HEAR IT?

(*Animals raise heads a little.*)

Can you hear it?

(*Faint Drip! Drip! can be heard.*)

ALL ANIMALS (*shivering and shaking*) YES! YES!

MRS NOAH It's getting louder, AND LOUDER, A N D L O U D E R!

(*Drip gradually gets louder.*)

DIFFERENT VOICES   Help! HELP!
SAVE US!
Save us, Mrs Noah!

(*Dripping sounds continue.*)

MRS NOAH   Save you? Save you from what?

ALL ANIMALS   CONSTANTDRIPPING!

MRS NOAH   Oh, that! All right! (*calls*) Noah! Ham! Plug that little hole in the roof of the Ark where the rain is coming in.

NOAH   (*calls*) All right! (*Dripping sounds stop.*)

HAM   (*calls*) Is that better?

MRS NOAH   MUCH BETTER! Well now, my dear animals . . . Don't you think that's better?

(NOAH *and* HAM *enter.*)

You'll never believe it, but the sound of that rain that CONSTANT . . . DRIPPING has really frightened these poor, dear animals of ours.

NOAH   And a very good thing too, if it's made them a bit quieter!

(*All animals realise the trick and mime their reactions.*)

MRS NOAH   Never mind! Never mind! Let's have a sing-along
while the Noah family gives out the rations.

(Buns are tossed to 'All Aboard' animals.)

ALL COMPANY

1 And so we sailed on night and day,
  Rock an' roll an' rock.
  And this old Ark did swing and sway,
  Rock an' roll an' rock.
  Chorus
  Rock an' roll
  Aboard the floating Zoo,
  Rock an' roll
  Aboard the floating Zoo.

*(During this verse and
chorus all casts from
other plays file across
Ark eating their buns
and waving.)*

2 And then at last, to their great joy,
  Rock an' roll an' rock.
  Old Noah called out, 'Land Ahoy!'
  Rock an' roll an' rock.

  Chorus

*(Noah climbs to high
point behind Ark.)*

3 'There's Land A'hoy!' they all did
  shout,
  Rock an' roll an' rock.
  Then two by two they all trooped
  out,
  Rock an' roll an' rock.
  Chorus

(Repeat as necessary.)

*(All start to move out,
singing.)*

The 'All Aboard' Song

The No-ahs built a gi-ant Ark, Rock an' roll 'an rock.

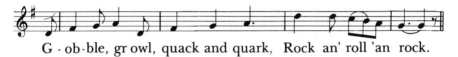

G-ob-ble, growl, quack and quark, Rock an' roll 'an rock.

Chorus

Rock an' roll A board the float-ing Zoo.

Rock an' roll A board the float-ing Zoo.

2 The animals came in two by two,
  Rock an' roll an' rock.
  The Noahs cried, 'What shall we do?'
  Rock an' roll an' rock.

  Chorus

3 The animals came in four by four,
  Rock an' roll an' rock.
  The Noahs cried, 'Let's shut the
  door!'
  Rock an' roll an' rock.

  Chorus

Suggestions for the Playmakers

or decorated skull cap

scarf tied at back

If you are a member of the Noah family you can dress like this.

Man　　　**Woman**

You can make an Ark shape like this.

'All Aboard' animals sit on forms across the back of the arena

EEP WAY AR

KEEP IN TWOS

NO BIRDS ON GANGWAY

HORNED ANIMALS ONLY

LIGHT WEIGHT ANIMALS ONLY

NO ANIM

1　　2　　3　　4

Nail hooks onto empty barrels or borrow P.E. equipment posts. Bind curtain rings onto the ends of rope or strong cord. These can be looped over the hooks or posts to make the shape of the Ark, and the rope can be dropped for entry of the animals.

Numbers 2 and 3 can be moved to the side during the three plays.

You can make animal head-dresses like this.

Use an old hat as a base. Get some thick wool or string.
Sew round the edge of the hat, making big loops as you go.
Sew more loops round the crown.
Cut the loops when you have finished making them.

You can make horns with an egg carton, playdough and thin elastic.

First make the playdough. Put one cup of water, one cup of flour,
half a cup of salt, one tablespoon of cooking oil and two teaspoons
of cream of tartar into a saucepan and stir. Heat the mixture gently.
Keep stirring until the mixture is thick. Leave to cool.

Cut two cups from the egg
carton. Stand them upside
down on paper.

Shape the playdough into the
horn shape on top of the cups.

Coat the sides of the base with
playdough and shape them.

Leave to set, then punch two
holes in the base of each horn
with a nail.

Thread elastic through the
holes and tie onto the hairy
head-dress.

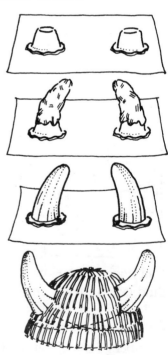